DOES
GRACE
GROW BEST
IN WINTER?

DOES
GRACE
GROW BEST
IN WINTER?

LIGON DUNCAN

WITH J. NICHOLAS REID

P&R
PUBLISHING
P.O. BOX 817 • PHILLIPSBURG • NEW JERSEY 08865-0817

Unless otherwise indicated, Scripture quotations are from The Holy Bible, English Standard Version, copyright © 2001 by Crossway Bibles, a division of Good News Publishers. Used by permission. All rights reserved.

Printed in the United States of America

Library of Congress Cataloging-in-Publication Data

Duncan, J. Ligon, 1960–
  Does grace grow best in winter? / Ligon Duncan ; with J. Nicholas Reid.
    p. cm.
  Includes bibliographical references.
  ISBN 978-1-59638-155-1 (pbk.)
  1. Suffering—Religious aspects—Christianity. 2. Providence and government of God—Christianity. I. Reid, J. Nicholas, 1979– II. Title.
  BV4909.D86 2009
  248.8'6—dc22
                                        2009015321

CONTENTS

PREFACE

WHILE I WAS ATTENDING the funeral of a friend who had died in a car wreck, I overheard the presiding minister—who, by the way, never knew my friend—say to some mourners in a condescending tone before the service began, "You know this is a joyous occasion, as well." On the one hand, the minister was correct. When a believer dies and goes to be with the Lord, there is cause for joy. The problem, on the other hand, comes when we act as if grief and sorrow are somehow sub-Christian emotions.

But that is not how the Bible handles suffering. The Bible consistently addresses the issue of suffering with the sincerity such a topic deserves, all the while offering gospel balm and comfort to the soul of the sufferer.

The problem with the way many Christians treat suffering is that they simply attempt to put a happy face on trials. A little personal suffering, however, goes a long way in revealing how vacuous careless platitudes can be. The issue of suffering is not to be treated in a cold and pedantic manner. Suffering is real and not something to be handled several steps removed. Yet if we address suffering merely subjectively, without focusing on the objective truths of the Bible, then there is all the reason in the world to despair.

Does Grace Grow Best in Winter? attempts to navigate these choppy waters and handle the issue of suffering as the Bible does, recognizing the difficulty of suffering, but also seeing a sovereign and good God at work in the midst of hardship.

A number of people have helped us with this book along the way and deserve our thanks. We would like to thank Dr. Guy Waters for reading an early version of this work and offering helpful feedback. We also thank Weezie Polk and Shirley Windham for reading the manuscript, and Donna Dobbs for crafting the study questions. Furthermore, we thank the session and members of First Presbyterian Church, Jackson, Mississippi, where these chapters were delivered by Ligon Duncan in lecture form. Finally, we thank Marvin Padgett, Thom Notaro, and the dear folks at P&R Publishing for taking on this work.

Our prayer is that God will use this study to enable his people to glorify and enjoy him even in the midst of suffering.

J. Nicholas Reid

I

WHY ME?

THIS BOOK CONSIDERS suffering in light of the sovereignty of our wise and loving God.[1] Since we believe that God causes all things to work together for good to those who love him, who are called according to his purpose (Romans 8:28), we will ask, How does God intend suffering to work for his children's good? God doesn't waste the suffering of his children, so how does he use suffering? In what ways do we grow in suffering? How do we respond to suffering?

We begin with the quandary of suffering: Why is there pain and sorrow in the first place? We live in a world of hurt. It is a constant. If we were able to know for a split second all the hardship that people face in this world at any given time, it would probably drive us mad. Only God could take in such knowledge without going insane.

Today three thousand little children will die of malaria, most of them in Africa. There will be numerous mothers and fathers bereft by the loss of their children because of this one disease.

This year alone, 1.5 million people will die in Africa because of AIDS. Fifty million people die every year, many of disease, and most young and in agony. One hundred people have died since you began reading this book. Think of the pain their loved ones feel in the wake of those deaths.

A little closer to home, you yourself may be suffering because of family issues. Perhaps estrangement from a parent has haunted you all your life, leaving you with the longing for a father or a mother to say just once, "I love you, and I'm proud of you. You bring me great joy and delight." But it never comes.

Perhaps you are a parent loving and caring for your child, all the while that child is making self-destructive choices that will have disastrous effects on his or her future. As a parent, you are doing the best you can. You are helping and counseling, but ultimately, there is nothing more that you can do except watch and pray.

Maybe the problem is with your marriage. You would never have dreamed that your marriage would break up, yet it has. Sometimes it happens for reasons that are understandable, and other times not. Either way the heartbreak is unbearable.

Suffering is such a part of this life that there is no way we could even begin to touch on every possible scenario.

SUFFERING HAPPENS

We need to learn that suffering happens. Or more specifically, suffering is to be expected. It is the norm in this fallen world. Many people claiming to be Christian teachers say that suffering should not be happening to you. But the Bible and experience prove that suffering is the norm in this fallen creation. In the world that God originally made there was no suffering, but our world is filled with it because sin brought suffering in its wake.

Understanding that suffering happens is important, not only because there are some who tell us that suffering should not to be a part of the Christian experience, but also because we have, by and large, been spared many of the trials that the rest of humanity has had to face. For instance, most of us have never lived through a famine, but up until the twentieth century most people would have lived through a number of them.

Since we live during a time in which some of the sufferings of this world have been mitigated for us, we are lulled to sleep sometimes and are surprised by suffering. When pain comes into our experience, our initial reaction is, "Oh, this shouldn't be happening!" But if what I am saying is true (that suffering is, that suffering happens, that suffering is the norm for this fallen world), none of us should ever be surprised by suffering. Instead, when it comes our way, we ought to be saying: "I've been waiting and preparing for you. I knew you were coming, because this fallen world is full of the likes of you. I've been preparing, by God's grace and by God's Word, to glorify God as I experience you." We must get it ingrained into our minds that suffering is an essential part of the Christian experience. You will suffer. That's the first thing you need to know. The question remains, will you suffer in a way that honors Christ?

LEARNING TO SUFFER WELL

Christians need to learn to suffer well. In order to do so, we need to consider what the Bible teaches Christians to do in the midst of suffering.

Admiral Nelson won the great Battle of Trafalgar against the French during the Napoleonic Wars. The Viscount of Camperdown, who also won many battles during that period, was one of the admirals under Nelson. The Viscount of Camperdown's family crest had a ship with full sails on it and with two little Latin words: *Disce pati*—"Learn to suffer." That is precisely what Peter and Paul and Job and Moses and Jesus would say to you and me as believers in this fallen world. "Learn to suffer."

What do I mean by that? Let me put some feet on it by offering five things in particular you and I need to learn about how to suffer.

1. Magnify Jesus. You must learn to suffer in such a way that Jesus is magnified in your difficulty. If you do not approach suffering with a desire for Jesus to be magnified, then you will encounter some hardship in this world that will completely overwhelm you because of its magnitude. When you are facing a long and enduring struggle, you need to be equipped with something bigger to fight against it, and there is nothing bigger than the glory of Jesus Christ. Your desire to see Jesus magnified is one of your great weapons in the war against suffering. You must learn how to suffer in such a way that Christ will be great in your eyes and in the eyes of all who see your suffering.

2. Love him more. Learn to suffer in such a way that Jesus becomes more precious to you than before. If you endure suffering, and Jesus is not more precious to you on the other side, then your suffering has not yet come to full fruition. Every single experience, good or ill, is designed by our loving heavenly Father to cause us to prize Jesus Christ more and more.

3. Know that God is for you. You need to learn to suffer in absolute confidence that God is for you. But I should qualify this statement. If you are trusting in Jesus Christ for salvation as he is offered in the gospel, you can endure suffering in absolute confidence that God is for you. Do not take my word for it. I am saying it on the authority of God's Word. You need to learn to suffer in full confidence that God is for you and that nothing can happen to you apart from his will.

Jesus made this point to his disciples in his Sermon on the Mount. Paul made this point to the suffering Christians in Romans 8. Peter made this point to the Christians who were getting ready to experience a great empire-wide persecution. You need to know that even in your darkest days God is still 100 percent for you. He is not against you, and everything that you need to endure, you already possess in Christ Jesus. But this truth is easier to say than it is to believe. It is easier to profess the truth than it is to rest in the truth during some difficult and dark time. But you need to begin a journey toward fully embracing it even in your darkest hour.

4. Rest on grace. Suffering does not gain you acceptance from God. Learn to suffer knowing that you are accepted by grace through faith, apart from anything that you do either before or after your conversion. There are some people who, for a variety of reasons, seem to think that if they just endure enough suffering, God will love them a little more. Such a perspective fails to recognize that God has loved his people with an everlasting love and that acceptance by him is not a result of our deeds or our suffering. We are accepted only because of Christ and his work on our behalf; this is important for us to understand in the midst of suffering. During intense and long suffering, the mind can become numb and begin to think all sorts of crazy things. If there is even a hint of doubt in the back of your mind about how you stand accepted with God, Satan will use it to undermine your comfort and assurance as you face suffering.

5. Embrace suffering. Learn to embrace a life of suffering. Paul describes himself as "sorrowful, yet always rejoicing" (2 Corinthians 6:10a). If we are a band of brothers and sisters over whom the banner is unfurled and flowing, "Suffering, yet rejoicing," there is no telling the gospel witness and effect it will have on the world around us. Talk about shaking the world out of its slumber—if we were a band of brothers and sisters in Christ dying yet living, suffering yet rejoicing, sorrowful yet full of inexpressible joy, what a comfort it would be to us, what a glory it would be to God, and what a witness it would be to the world. Be prepared to embrace a life of suffering.

BALM FOR THE SUFFERING SOUL

The good news if you are suffering today is that the Bible says so much about what you are going through. I've had the privilege—and I really mean *privilege*—of talking with many people in my church who have suffered through things that I have never experienced. During those times, if all I had to say to those individuals came from my own wisdom, books, or my meager experience, it would be utterly pathetic and depressing. But thank the Lord that you do not have to rely on my wisdom or common sense or experience, or anyone else's for that matter. Instead, the Word of God is waiting with wisdom and comfort for you in the midst of your difficulty. God has said much in his Word to you about your suffering, and it is my inestimable privilege of opening up his Word and saying, "Friend, look at the feast of help that God has prepared for you in his Word. It does not come from me! It does not come from my experience. It does not come from my wisdom. It comes from God!"

Let me just give you some hors d'oeuvres of how much God says in the Bible about suffering. "Therefore you gave them into the hand of their enemies, who made them suffer. And in the time of their suffering they cried out to you and you heard them from heaven, and according to your great mercies you gave them saviors who saved them from the hand of their enemies" (Nehemiah 9:27). God heard and answered their prayers in the midst of their suffering.

"More than that, we rejoice in our sufferings, knowing that suffering produces endurance, and endurance produces character, and character produces hope, and hope does not put us to shame, because God's love has been poured into our hearts through the Holy Spirit who has been given to us" (Romans 5:3–5). Paul unveils the truth that believers are able to rejoice in their sufferings!

In Ephesians 3:13, Paul says to the dear Christians in Ephesus, who loved him so deeply, "So I ask you not to lose heart over what I am suffering for you, which is your glory." From this passage, I think I could prove to you not only that the suffering of the servants of Christ—those whom God has appointed as the ministers of the Word—is intended for the benefit of God's people, but also that all of your sufferings, collectively, are meant for the benefit of one another. Your suffering, friend in Christ, is meant for the strengthening of your faith, as well as others around you. This means that we really do not want to miss anything that God intends for us to gain corporately through suffering.

Since Ephesians 3:13 is true, personal testimonies can be heartening in the local church. It is an enormous blessing to see the hand of God's grace at work in a fellow believer. God doesn't waste that suffering, and we should not either.

The book of 2 Timothy has a lot to say about suffering.

> Therefore do not be ashamed of the testimony about our Lord, nor of me his prisoner, but share in suffering for the gospel by the power of God, who saved us and called us to a holy calling, not because of our works but because of his own purpose and grace, which he gave us in Christ Jesus before the ages began. (2 Timothy 1:8-9)

Paul is saying in effect, "Look, when somebody says, 'Since your Savior died on a cross and your apostolic hero is in prison, your religion must be false,' don't be discouraged. Don't be ashamed when you tell them that you worship a crucified Savior and that the minister you support is chained to a Roman guard." Paul also says, "Share in suffering as a good soldier of Christ

Jesus" (2 Timothy 2:3); "As for you, always be sober-minded, endure suffering . . ." (2 Timothy 4:5).

Or consider Hebrews 2:10: "For it was fitting that he, for whom and by whom all things exist, in bringing many sons to glory, should make the founder of their salvation perfect through suffering." Jesus was made perfect through suffering? The heavenly Father has appointed the captain of our salvation to be made perfect through suffering. This is simply astounding.

The list continues. "As an example of suffering and patience, brothers, take the prophets who spoke in the name of the Lord" (James 5:10). "Is anyone among you suffering? Let him pray" (James 5:13).

> For this is a gracious thing, when, mindful of God, one endures sorrows while suffering unjustly. For what credit is it if when you sin and are beaten for it you endure? But when you do good and suffer for it, this is a gracious thing in the sight of God. For to this you have been called, because Christ also suffered for you, leaving you an example, so that you might follow in his steps. (1 Peter 2:19–21)

> Resist [the devil], firm in your faith, knowing that the same kinds of suffering are being experienced by your brotherhood throughout the world. And after you have suffered a little while, the God of all grace, who has called you to his eternal glory in Christ, will

himself restore, confirm, strengthen, and establish you. (1 Peter 5:9–10)

Those are just a few hors d'oeuvres of how much God has given to us in the Bible by the inspiration of the Holy Spirit. Isn't that comforting to you? We live in a world of constant suffering, but God has graciously spoken to us about it in numerous places in his Word.

One of the proofs that this is God's Word is that it says so much to us about suffering. The Lord cares about his children. Thus, he wants us to know the truth. He wants us to be comforted by the truth.

THE CAUSES OF SUFFERING

The causes of suffering can be summed up in three words: sin, Satan, and God. The first can be subdivided so that we have four grand categories to explain why we experience suffering in this world: our sin, the sins of others, Satan's activity, and our sovereign God. Frequently, suffering is caused by not just one, but a combination of these categories.

For instance, in 1 Chronicles 21, David, the king of Israel, orders a census to be taken of the people. You might be tempted to think that this action is insignificant. But God explicitly told the kings of Israel not to take a census. This was to remind them that Israel's security was not based on the number of fighting-aged males. Israel's security, rather, was based on God's protection. God wanted the king and all the people to trust in him alone and not in military might. David, however, breaks God's law and takes a census. This has dire consequences for the people of God. Tens of thousands of people end up suffering because of David's choice to have a census. First Chronicles 21:1 states, "Then Satan stood against Israel and incited David to number Israel." The author of Chronicles tells us that Satan was behind this temptation. So, the suffering that Israel experienced was the result of David's sin and Satan's activity.

But look at 2 Samuel 24:1–2:

Again the anger of the LORD was kindled against Israel, and he incited David against them, saying, "Go, number Israel and Judah." So the king said to Joab, the commander of the army, who was with him, "Go through all the tribes of Israel, from Dan to Beersheba, and number the people, that I may know the number of the people."

Wait a minute! Satan is the one who tempted David to take that census, and yet 2 Samuel says that God was angry with Israel and incited David to take the census. What's going on here? God is sovereign. Satan is active. Man is sinful. David does exactly what he wants to do. Satan does exactly what he wants to do. And God sovereignly appoints all things according to his own will. All of these things are a part of the suffering that was experienced in Israel.

Another example is from Job 1:

> Now there was a day when the sons of God came to present themselves before the LORD, and Satan also came among them. The LORD said to Satan, "From where have you come?" Satan answered the LORD and said, "From going to and fro on the earth, and from walking up and down on it." And the LORD said to Satan, "Have you considered my servant Job, that there is none like him on the earth, a blameless and upright man, who fears God and turns away from evil?" (verses 6–8)

In this passage, it is not Satan who comes to God and says, "Hey, I'd like to take out Job at the knees." Instead, God in effect says, "I see you've been roaming the earth. Let me mention somebody to you, somebody whom I love, somebody who loves me. His name's Job. Have you thought about him much, Satan?" Satan basically says, "Now that you mention it, I believe if he were ever afflicted and all the blessings that you've given him were taken away, he would curse you to your face, because you're not worth living for." God disagrees. And the rest is literally history.

In that great book of the Bible we are told that Job's sins have absolutely nothing to do with his trials. Sure, he struggled with sin and unbelief during his trials, but Job's sin had absolutely nothing to do with causing his trials. Satan was active in them, and God was sovereign over them.

As we think about the causes of suffering in this world, we first have to think about sin. There would be no suffering in this world if there were no sin. In Genesis 3:15–17, God says that pain and toil will come into this world because of Adam's sin. There would be no suffering in this world, were it not for sin, which is one of the great lessons of suffering. Always draw a line back from suffering to sin. The point is not necessarily that *my* suffering is because of something that I have done. Rather, in the face of suffering, learn to hate sin like we all hate suffering. This should be easy because there would be no suffering in this world had Adam not sinned.

Of course, much of the suffering in this world does result from our own sin. I suspect that most of the suffering I experience is the result of my own sin. Sometimes suffering is caused by personal sin, and sometimes it is caused by the sins of others. Sometimes suffering is the result of the work of Satan, but over it all, God is always sovereign.

When suffering comes knocking at your door, God does not take a step back and say, "You're on your own. This is outside the sphere of my ability, competence, and sovereignty." If that were the case, then in the very place where you need God most, he would not be there. It is much better to be left with the question in the night, "What in the world are you doing, Lord?" than to think, "You know, I cannot ask the Lord what he is doing, because he is not in this. I am on my own." I would rather be asking, "What in the world are you doing, Lord?" than to think God can't do anything about this because he is not in it.

Nowhere in the book of Job does he say, "Lord, couldn't you help me here, but I know you can't." Rather, Job says in essence, "Lord, I know you are in control. Why are you doing this?" Job asks this because God is in charge of everything, which means that when we are experiencing suffering, we have Someone to whom we can turn. As much comfort as we may get from friends in this world—and we need all the comfort we can get—there is no one who knows our suffering like God. This book is about what he has to say to us in our darkest hours of need.

STUDY QUESTIONS

1. How did humankind become subject to suffering (Genesis 3; Romans 5:12–21; 1 Corinthians 15:21)?

2. To what extent are we still affected by that original act (Romans 8:18–21)?

   a. Be specific about its ramifications in human nature and even the physical world in which we live.

   b. What kind of conditions exist not as the result of personal sin, but as a result of the fall?

3. Although difficult and even painful, not all suffering is bad. The greatest blessing for a person is not freedom from pain; instead, the greatest blessing is to be more like Christ. God can use trials and suffering to cause us to become more like his Son. What does Romans 8:28–29 teach us about understanding our experience of suffering?

4. Paul was no stranger to suffering. What can you learn from Paul's autobiographical statements about his suffering (2 Corinthians 4:8–10; 12:7; Romans 5:3–5)?

5. There are many different reasons for suffering. As we have seen, some are the result of living in a fallen world, and not because of any particular action of our own. Sometimes, however, we bring

suffering on ourselves. List some of the reasons given in these passages (Nehemiah 9:26–27; Psalm 107:17; Proverbs 11:24; 13:20; 19:15; 22:3; Jeremiah 13:22).

6. Jesus came into this world to defeat Satan and the effects of the sin that causes our suffering. Read Hebrews 2 and explain how he did that.

2

WHAT IS GOD UP TO?

IT WOULD BE terrible if God's Word did not speak to us about suffering. Isn't it heartening that God spends so much time in his Word speaking to us about such an important and constant part of our experience, one in which we all need help? The harder suffering gets and the longer it lasts, the more confused we can become. In those times we especially need the clarity of God's Word speaking into our lives and hearts.

As we've seen, there are different causes of suffering. We acknowledged that our sin causes suffering. But it is important to understand that this does *not* mean you can make the equation, "I'm suffering, so God therefore is punishing me for a sin that I have committed." That may be true in some instances, but it is not always true. God wants us to look at more than just personal sin as the cause of suffering.

Genesis 3 records that human sin brought suffering into this world. God told Eve that because of her sin she would experience pain in bearing children. God told Adam that because of his sin he would experience toil and frustration as he attempted to work. God, then, made it clear that the toil, pain, misery, and suffering of life that we all experience in this fallen world are the result of Adam and Eve's sin. Suffering would not have come into the world had they not been unfaithful to God. But it is not just that Adam and Eve have sinned. All of us are inclined to sin, and our sin sometimes brings us suffering.

In 1 Peter 2:19–22, Peter encourages Christians to endure suffering.

For this is a gracious thing, when, mindful of God, one endures sorrows while suffering unjustly. For what credit is it if, when you sin and are beaten for it, you endure? But if when you do good and suffer for it you endure, this is a gracious thing in the sight of God. For to this you have been called, because Christ also suffered for you, leaving you an example, so that you might follow in his steps. He committed no sin, neither was deceit found in his mouth.

We noted in chapter 1 that sometimes suffering is the result of our own sin. Other times it is the direct result of the sins of others. You may know what it's like to carry around hurts and pains, unfulfilled desires, and heartbreaks because of something you experienced as a child, perhaps even at the hands of your own parents. Suffering is not necessarily your fault. It may very well result from the sins of others.

We saw too that suffering is frequently the result of satanic activity, as it was in Job's day. Satan was behind the sufferings that Job experienced. It was not that Job had sinned and God was punishing him as a result. Rather, Satan desired to sift Job like wheat, causing him to suffer.

Ultimately, however, suffering is under the sovereignty of God. As we saw before, some people do not want to think that God is involved in their suffering. It is so painful, they cannot conceive of a good and loving God having anything to do with it. In order to protect the goodness of God, they, ironically, push him as far away as they can from their suffering. But think about it—if God is removed from suffering, then our painful experiences, which generate some of the most significant moments we have in this life, are outside the reach of our God. That is not very encouraging at all. I want God right in the middle of my suffering. But it's not just a matter of what I want; it's about what the Bible says. God is sovereign even over suffering.

What Is God up to in Your Suffering?

If God is sovereign over your suffering, then what in the world are his purposes in all of it? We will look at four things that God says he intends to accomplish through our suffering.

Teaching Us Godliness

What are the divine and good purposes of suffering? God tells us in his Word that he purposes to work godliness in us through suffering. "More than that, we rejoice in our sufferings, knowing that suffering produces endurance, and endurance produces character, and character produces hope, and hope does not put us to shame, because God's love has been poured into our hearts through the Holy Spirit who has been given to us" (Romans 5:3–5). Although there is no way we can exhaust the riches of its meaning, let me in one sentence try to sum up what Paul is saying: God ordains for your suffering to produce endurance, character, and hope.

In other words, suffering is an instrument in the hands of God's Holy Spirit to build up believers in godliness. This can give us joy in the midst of trials. We do not rejoice in suffering because we are masochists. We rejoice in our sufferings because we know that God the Holy Spirit is working in us according to his sovereign plan. God uses suffering to build something in us that would not have been there otherwise. God uses suffering to grow his church in godliness.

You can see this reality among your Christian friends who have suffered the most. It has not made them bitter; rather, they have become much sweeter. Not only are they sweeter; they are stronger too. They have already looked death in the face and have not flinched, so no matter what comes their way, they are going to be okay. And it is your joy, as a friend, to see God at work producing character in them.

On the other hand, you have probably seen your unbelieving friends meet the same suffering that your believing friends have, yet it has made them smaller and more brittle and bitter. Suffering does not produce godliness in and of itself. It is the Holy Spirit at work in you who uses suffering to make you grow in grace. That is why the same suffering bears entirely different fruit in those who by faith trust in Christ than in those who do not. The Holy Spirit uses our suffering to produce in us endurance, character, and hope. That's the first purpose of suffering.

Giving Us Surpassing Joy in Christ

God uses suffering to cause us to prize Christ more than this world. From the time you were in Sunday school, you have probably been told that the letter to the Philippians was "the letter of joy." Your teachers were exactly right. I do not know a smaller book in the New Testament that talks more about suffering than Philippians, yet it is the letter of joy. Joy in the midst of suffering is not a contradiction in Christianity. It may be a contradiction in the eyes of the world, but for the believer, rejoicing and suffering can go in the same sentence without fear of contradiction. Isn't it glorious that we can turn to Philippians, that book of joy, to learn about suffering? Paul says:

> Indeed, I count everything as loss because of the surpassing worth of knowing Christ Jesus my Lord. For his sake I have suffered the loss of all things and count them as rubbish, in order that I may gain Christ and be found in him, not having a righteousness of my own that comes from the law, but that which comes through faith in Christ, the righteousness from God that depends on faith—that I may know him and the power of his resurrection, and may share his sufferings, becoming like him in his death, that by any means possible I may attain the resurrection from the dead. (Philippians 3:8–11)

God ordains that our suffering will, by the Holy Spirit and by faith, produce in us the right estimate of both the ephemeral treasures of this world and an eternal knowledge of Jesus Christ. Suffering gives us a correct estimate of the things of this life: they are passing away. Before we are suffering, we deeply enjoy them. But in our suffering they are not so enticing anymore. As the pleasures of this world fade in our estimation, the salvation of Jesus Christ is magnified.

Paul is basically saying, "Look, here's what happened with me. I was a respected religious leader in Judaism. I was an up and comer. I was seen as a future leader of my people, a moral leader of my people over against the pagan influences of Rome. But as I was on my way to Damascus to persecute the church, I met Jesus. In that moment, I lost everything. And praise God for it!" Everything Paul esteemed was taken from him that day, yet he received the One who is the fairest of ten thousand, the Lord Jesus Christ.

God ordains by his Holy Spirit that our suffering will make clear to us both the passing treasures of this world and the surpassing greatness of the joy of knowing Jesus Christ.

A friend of mine lost her two-year-old child to a drowning accident in the family pool. As she held him in her arms while his life slipped away at the hospital, she looked up to me and said, "Ligon, could we sing

'The Doxology' now?" In the midst of her grief, she knew that her son would not return to her, but she would one day go to be with him. So, she wanted to sing "The Doxology" to her Creator as the very last breath of her child slipped away. She prized Christ more than anything else, and through the crucible of her suffering, the Holy Spirit worked a deeper faith into her.

God purposes to use our suffering to cause us to treasure the things of this world less and to treasure the eternal fellowship we have with Jesus Christ more than all this world has to offer.

Building up the Church

Our suffering aids the maturity of the whole body of believers. It is extraordinary that our suffering is designed not only to work godliness in us as individuals, causing us to prize Christ more, but also to work maturity within the whole church. Paul says in Colossians 1:24–29:

> Now I rejoice in my sufferings for your sake, and in my flesh I am filling up what is lacking in Christ's afflictions for the sake of his body, that is, the church, of which I became a minister according to the stewardship from God that was given to me for you, to make the word of God fully known, the mystery hidden for

ages and generations but now revealed to his saints. To them God chose to make known how great among the Gentiles are the riches of the glory of this mystery, which is Christ in you, the hope of glory. Him we proclaim, warning everyone and teaching everyone with all wisdom, that we may present everyone mature in Christ. For this I toil, struggling with all his energy that he powerfully works within me.

Suffering is God's instrument to bring about the maturity of the whole church. God ordains for our suffering, as a participation in the suffering of Christ's body, to bring about in the church the purposes of Christ's affliction. In other words, sometimes God appoints his children to suffer so that the whole body will become mature.

These "lacking" afflictions of Christ's do not indicate that his suffering was insufficient for our salvation. They are simply a recognition that when you become a believer in the Lord Jesus Christ, you become a part of his body. Since you are part of his body, your sufferings are his sufferings. What are the sufferings that are lacking in Christ's affliction? They are the ones that have not been experienced yet by his body, the church. They will continue to be experienced by his body until he comes again and makes an end of all suffering for his people.

The apostle Paul is telling us something amazing. The afflictions of the body of Christ are intended to bring it to maturity. That is to say, God ordains, by the Spirit and by faith, for our suffering to bring about in the church the purposes of Christian affliction. These purposes are: Christ in us, the hope of glory, and every one of us being made mature in Jesus Christ.

Several years ago, my wife and I had the privilege of going to Vienna, Austria, to work with some missionaries who were serving mostly in eastern Europe, but would come to Vienna for missionary training. A number of them were taking courses with Reformed Theological Seminary (while I was still teaching at the seminary). My job was to teach the doctrine of God to about seven veteran missionaries, one of whom was Dave Babcock.

During the lunch break on the second day of class, we started talking about what some of them did. It turned out that Dave was a colleague of Brother Andrew, the missionary famous for smuggling Bibles into Communist countries, as told in the book *God's Smuggler*. Dave in fact did most of the things described in the book, but the authors could not name him for fear of Communist bloc persecution. Dave had already been arrested, imprisoned, and beaten in Bulgaria, Turkey, Ukraine, Russia, China, and many other places that I've forgotten. He was very reticent to talk about any of this, but as I drew information out of him, something kept crossing my mind: "Should I be standing in a class telling Dave Babcock what to believe about God and Jesus and how to serve the Lord? Dave, come up and teach the class! I'm sitting down from now on!" There's nothing that will humble you more quickly than somebody who has served the Lord so faithfully.

Late on the first full day, Anne and I got to the home where we were staying, and our hosts started bringing us dinner. The meal was very simple, made up of small portions. First, they served Anne and me, giving us what I thought were little portions. Inside I was thinking, "You know, I've been traveling, and I'm kind of hungry here. But all I'm getting is a biscuit and some old milk." But when they got around the room, I realized that two of their children were not eating. They were not eating because their portions had been given to Anne and me, and there was no other food in the house.

I began shrinking, so it seemed. "What am I doing teaching these folks about God and the Bible," I thought. But God used their suffering to build me up and strengthen me in the faith. I just wanted to be around them and Dave and to have the privilege of talking with someone who had loved his Savior to the point of enduring beatings and persecution and humiliation, had taken Bible after Bible after Bible into the Communist bloc, had shared Christ, was giving the whole of his life, and was living in poverty for the sake of the gospel. It was like food for my soul just to be around him.

I have never forgotten that week. I may never get to fellowship with Dave Babcock again in this life, but I will never forget him and the gift that he gave me through his suffering.

Your suffering does not just belong to you. You are members of a body. Your suffering is for the body's maturing as much as it is for yours. Your suffering is there to build up the church of Christ. It is there for the people of God to be given faith and hope and confidence in the hour of their trials. Your suffering is also the body's suffering because one of God's purposes in suffering is the maturity of the whole church.

Preparing Us for Glory

God's purpose in our suffering is to prepare us for glory.

> But we have this treasure in jars of clay, to show that the surpassing power belongs to God and not to us. We are afflicted in every way, but not crushed; perplexed, but not driven to despair; persecuted, but not forsaken; struck down, but not destroyed; always

carrying in the body the death of Jesus, so that the life of Jesus may also be manifested in our bodies. For we who live are always being given over to death for Jesus' sake, so that the life of Jesus also may be manifested in our mortal flesh. So death is at work in us, but life in you.

Since we have the same spirit of faith according to what has been written, "I believed, and so I spoke," we also believe, and so we also speak, knowing that he who raised the Lord Jesus will raise us also with Jesus and bring us with you into his presence. For it is all for your sake, so that as grace extends to more and more people it may increase thanksgiving, to the glory of God.

So we do not lose heart. Though our outer self is wasting away, our inner self is being renewed day by day. For this light momentary affliction is preparing for us an eternal weight of glory beyond all comparison, as we look not to the things that are seen but to the things that are unseen. For the things that are seen are transient, but the things that are unseen are eternal. (2 Corinthians 4:7–18)

Paul is saying that God ordains, by the Spirit and by faith, for our suffering to show us God's power in a way that we could not have seen it without having experienced such difficulty. Our suffering shows us God's power in our weakness, and it prepares us for an eternal weight of glory beyond all comparison. The only way I know even how to begin scratching the surface of what Paul is saying is to sum it up like this: You couldn't bear the glory that God has in store for you, unless you had been held up by God in your affliction in this life. The apostle Paul is telling you that your suffering is not just for now. It is not just for maturity in Christ—though it is for that. It is not just for godliness—though it is for that too. It is not just so that you'll prize Christ now, or for the edification of the body—though it is for those good purposes as well. Your suffering prepares you for a glory that you cannot even comprehend. If you were not being held up by God in your affliction now, you could not bear the glory that he is going to bestow upon you.

This takes us right back to Romans 5. There is a hope that cannot be taken from believers in suffering, because God is up to something bigger than us. We are going to participate in glory in such a way that we can describe our fellowship with him as joy inexpressible and full of glory. Such joy awaits all those who trust in Christ, no matter how much or how long they have suffered in this world. Even if you were to suffer every single moment of every single day for the rest of your life, each moment that you endure would bring you one moment closer to glory! Suffering will cease for the Christian, but glory goes on forever.

Study Questions

1. Since even our suffering is under the sovereignty of God, how does that comfort the Christian?

2. In what ways can a Christian grow through the things he or she suffers?

3. "Rejoicing in suffering" is not a contradiction to a Christian. Can you testify to times that you have experienced both joy and sorrow at the same time? Explain.

4. How can other Christians (the body of Christ) benefit from your trials? How have you benefited by observing your fellow Christians' response to suffering?

5. How can God's glory be magnified when Christians suffer?

3

HOW CAN WE PROFIT FROM SUFFERING?

PEOPLE HAVE WRITTEN three-, four-, and five-hundred-page books—good books!—on the benefits of suffering and have not exhausted the Bible's answer to this question. So, I am not pretending to deal with this subject exhaustively in any way. I merely want to suggest some places in God's Word where you can go for help in this area. I want to consider seven things that we can do as believers to profit most from our affliction.

BELIEVE IN GOD'S GOOD PURPOSES

"More than that, we rejoice in our sufferings, knowing that suffering produces endurance, and endurance produces character, and character produces hope, and hope does not put us to shame, because God's love has been poured into our hearts through the Holy Spirit who has been given to us" (Romans 5:3–5). The apostle Paul affirms at least two things in this passage. First, God has a good purpose in suffering. Paul's trials are designed to produce endurance and character and hope. But he also affirms his ability to rejoice *in* suffering, not necessarily *because* of suffering. Although you will find Paul later in the book of Acts confessing that he rejoices over the privilege to suffer for the Lord Jesus Christ, he is not saying that he enjoys the suffering in and of itself. God has a good purpose in our trials, so we must determine to rejoice even in our suffering.

Rely on God's Power

We must rely on the power of God and not on our own strength to face suffering. We prepare ourselves to profit most from our suffering if we face it in his power and not our own.

Paul says to Timothy,

Therefore do not be ashamed of the testimony about our Lord, nor of me his prisoner, but share in suffering for the gospel by the power of God, who saved us and called us to a holy calling, not because of our works but because of his own purpose and grace, which he gave us in Christ Jesus before the ages began. (2 Timothy 1:8–9)

The testimony that Paul is talking about is that Jesus has been crucified. Crucifixion was a humiliating thing. Perhaps Timothy encountered people who mocked him and his message by basically saying, "You're trying to sell me a crucified Savior? That's ridiculous! That's shameful! Furthermore, your God cannot be very great, your best guy, Paul, is in prison." Timothy may have been shaken up by this, and so Paul tells him not to be ashamed of serving and loving a crucified Lord.

If you are anything like me, the minute you find yourself in a corner, you begin trying to figure out how you are going to get out. Instead, you and I should be saying, "Lord God, by the grace of your Son, Jesus Christ, I'm your child. You care more about me than I care about myself. You care better for me than I care for myself. Help me. Guard my heart. Make sure that I don't try and find a way out of this mess and make things worse than they already are. I know that I can trust you." Paul is telling us to rely on the power of God when we face suffering.

Approach Suffering Like a Good Soldier

If we want to benefit most from our suffering, by prayer and meditation, we will approach our suffering as a good soldier approaches war. What do I mean by that? A good soldier who has trained and trained is not surprised when he finds himself in war! He has been trained for it. Likewise, consider it your job to be prepared to suffer. That puts a whole different cast on Sunday morning, doesn't it? You are gathering with God's people Lord's Day after Lord's Day to train as good soldiers of Jesus Christ so that when your time of trial and testing and suffering comes, you will be ready.

If we are going to benefit most from our suffering, we will approach our suffering as good soldiers would approach war. We need to consider it our job—not a surprise, not an interruption—to prepare for suffering. "Share in suffering as a good soldier of Christ Jesus," Paul says (2 Timothy 2:3). Paul wants us to think of ourselves as soldiers preparing for war, a war that will, for all of us in some measure and different ways, entail suffering. Approach it like a soldier with a resolve that says, "I'm being prepared for war. I'm not going to be surprised when the war comes. I'm being prepared for suffering. I won't be taken by surprise when the suffering comes."

Participate in Jesus' Suffering

If we are going to benefit most from our suffering by God's grace, we must consider that we are being drawn into the experience of Jesus Christ, for he himself was perfected in suffering. That is one reason why we will spend the last chapter dealing with the suffering of Christ. If we are, by grace through faith, part of the body of Christ, then we share in the sufferings of Christ. We do not share in his sufferings that purchased our redemption, that is, his sufferings by which we were accepted freely in the beloved, were justified, and were adopted as children of the living God. Rather, we share in the sufferings of his body because as the church, we are the body of Christ.

As the apostle was on the road to Damascus to persecute more Christians, Jesus appeared to him and said, "Saul! Saul! Why are you persecuting me?" (Acts 9:4). Why did Jesus say that? He said it because the church's sufferings are his sufferings, because the church is Jesus' body. To touch Jesus' body is to touch Jesus. When you suffer, you are participating in the sufferings of Christ. It is vital for us to understand what was taking place in his suffering.

The author of Hebrews contemplates this in Hebrews 2:10, "For it was fitting that he, for whom and by whom all things exist, in bringing many sons to glory, should

47

make the founder of their salvation perfect through suffering." For the rest of your life, you could meditate on the words that Jesus was made "perfect through suffering." How do you make the perfect, more perfect? Making perfect more perfect sounds absurd, but that is precisely what the author of Hebrews says. When a believer in the Lord Jesus Christ suffers, he or she is being drawn into the experience of Jesus Christ, for he himself was perfected through suffering.

Remember You Are Not Alone

If you are going to profit most from your suffering, by God's grace, then consider that you are not alone in your suffering, but in the company of the greatest of the saints.

James, addressing Christians who were enduring suffering, says, "As an example of suffering and patience, brothers, take the prophets who spoke in the name of the Lord" (James 5:10). James is in effect saying to these Jewish Christians who are suffering because of their faith, "Brothers, look at the example of the prophets who suffered for their loyalty to the Lord, who suffered for their faith. You are part of their same company. You're not suffering alone. You're part of a company of suffering believers."

Consider what Peter says in 1 Peter 5:9–10 to a whole different group of Christians in Asia Minor:

> Resist [the devil], firm in your faith, knowing that the same kinds of suffering are being experienced by your brotherhood throughout the world. And after you have suffered a little while, the God of all grace, who has called you to his eternal glory in Christ, will himself restore, confirm, strengthen, and establish you.

You are not alone in your suffering. In fact, when you begin to contemplate the suffering that has been and is being endured by your brethren, it is utterly humbling.

Recently in Turkey some Muslims cruelly tortured three missionaries who were distributing Bibles and Christian literature. The Muslims ended the lives of those missionaries by slitting their throats. Their wives and children are still alive, bearing the pain of the loss of their husbands and fathers. These are your brothers and sisters in Christ.

Whatever suffering you are facing, you endure it in solidarity with your brothers and sisters worldwide. You are not alone in your suffering; you are in the company of the greatest of saints, which is a humbling thought. In fact, most of our suffering is small in comparison to the suffering of the rest of the brotherhood and sisterhood of believers around the world.

Pray without Ceasing

James, under the inspiration of the Holy Spirit, gives us very simple and clear direction: "Is anyone among you suffering? Let him pray" (James 5:13). Suffering will be lost on us, if it does not drive us into the arms of Jesus. Suffering will be lost on us if we are separated from the one who ought to be the delight and desire of our soul. James says that if you are suffering, you must run to your heavenly Father, through the Son, by the Spirit. Run to the triune God! Do not cease or fail to pray in your suffering, or your suffering will fail to profit you.

Learn and Sing the Great Hymns of Suffering

If you want to learn to profit most from your suffering, by God's grace, learn and sing the great hymns of suffering. Are you wondering where I am going to get a verse for this one?

The apostle Paul, while writing to the Colossians, says, "Let the word of Christ dwell in you richly, teaching and admonishing one another in all wisdom, singing psalms and hymns and spiritual songs, with thankfulness in your hearts to God" (Colossians 3:16). Paul considers the very act of singing psalms and hymns and spiritual songs as a way of mutually encouraging one another to allow the word of Christ to dwell in them richly. If you want to learn to suffer so as to profit most by God's grace for God's purposes, learn and sing the great hymns of suffering.

"Commit Now All Your Griefs" may not be a familiar hymn. The words, nevertheless, are incredibly powerful. "Whate'er My God Ordains Is Right" is a great hymn to help you in times of trouble. "Though Troubles Assail Us, the Lord Will Provide" is another great hymn on which to meditate, as is "It Is Well with My Soul," "Be Still, My Soul," or one in an entirely different vein, "Am I a Soldier of the Cross?" A new song that is very helpful is "When Trials Come," by Keith and Kristyn Getty.

Learn and sing the great hymns of suffering. For example, sit down sometime with the hymn "If Thou but Suffer God to Guide Thee," by Georg Neumark, and see how profitable those lyrics are to the soul that is suffering. And as you meditate on its lyrics, you may be encouraged to know that the author of this hymn was not a "dry-land sailor." When he wrote about suffering, he understood more than a little about it.

The author was robbed by highwaymen near Magdeburg in Germany as a student, and he was left destitute, with no prospect of earning a living. He had been given funds to go off to university and set out with a group of travelers. Along the way robbers overtook the whole party of travelers in a valley and stole everything he had, leaving Neumark with no money to enroll in university. Physically assaulted, he no longer had any means for making a living. His whole life was changed by that single moment. Although he could have spent the rest of his life in bitterness, he did not. The Lord was kind to him, and Neumark was used to pen a song that has provided balm for many weary and suffering souls.

That is just one example of a song that the Lord has given to his church to sing in times of suffering. Meditating upon the great hymns of suffering will remind you that the very struggles you are going through now have been experienced by believing saints throughout the ages.

Set Your Heart on Getting the Most out of Suffering

We need to shift gears a little and ask, What state of the heart ought we to aim for in order to get the most out of suffering? You and I must humble ourselves before the Lord. "Humble yourselves, therefore, under the mighty hand of God so that at the proper time he may exalt you, casting all your anxieties on him, because he cares for you" (1 Peter 5:6–7). How do you humble yourself before the Lord, casting your worries on him while waiting for him to exalt you? Here are seven ways.

1. Let your heart be assured that there is no circumstance so overwhelming that God will not use it to do a work of grace in you.

We need to prayerfully meditate on and read the Scripture, until by faith we are assured that no circumstances are so overwhelming that God will not do a work of grace in our hearts through them. Consider these words of encouragement:

No temptation [no trial, no tribulation] has overtaken you that is not common to man. God is faithful, and he will not let you be tempted beyond your ability, but with the temptation he will also provide the way of escape, that you may be able to endure it. (1 Corinthians 10:13)

[God] said to me, "My grace is sufficient for you, for my power is made perfect in weakness." (2 Corinthians 12:9)

I can do all things through him who strengthens me.
(Philippians 4:13)

Pray, meditate, read, and trust until you are assured that
there are no circumstances that are so overwhelming
that God will not do a work of grace in your heart.

*2. Pray, meditate, read, and trust until you know
that whatever hand is in your suffering, God is
your help, and do not forget to rely on God for the
battle you are in.*

Micah 6:9 says, "The voice of the LORD cries to the
city—and it is sound wisdom to fear your name: 'Hear of
the rod and of him who appointed it!'" In other words,
Israel is going to be under the rod of discipline, but
Micah doesn't want the people of God to see only the
rod and miss the One who appointed it. In the midst
of their suffering, Micah wants Israel to have their eyes
fixed on God. Even if that rod is coming from a pagan,
enemy invader, ultimately God is in charge. Micah
doesn't want Israel to lose sight of God by focusing too
much on their trial. God is their help, no matter where
the suffering is coming from. So, whatever has caused
the suffering—your sin or someone else's sin, whether
the suffering is just or unjust, whether it's because of
natural acts or supernatural acts, wherever the suffering

has come from—God is your help. Don't lose God in the middle of the battle! Keep your eyes on him! Don't lose sight of him in the midst of the storm.

3. Pray, meditate, read, and believe until you are convinced of God's infinite greatness.

If our hearts would be right, and if we would suffer so as to profit most by God's grace for God's purposes, we'll pray and meditate and read and believe until we are convinced of God's infinite greatness.

Sometimes our suffering can seem greater than everything else, tempting us to see our circumstances as bigger than God. When we focus on the greatness of our suffering, we can forget that our God is bigger than any and every other thing we might have to face. We must, therefore, pray and meditate and read until we believe and are convinced that God is bigger than our suffering.

Isaiah 6 takes place during a time of national crisis, namely, the great king Uzziah has died.

> In the year that King Uzziah died I saw the Lord sitting upon a throne, high and lifted up; and the train of his robe filled the temple. Above him stood the seraphim. Each had six wings: with two he covered his face, and with two he covered his feet, and with two he flew. And one called to another and said:

"Holy, holy, holy is the LORD of hosts;
  the whole earth is full of his glory!"

And the foundations of the thresholds shook at the voice of him who called, and the house was filled with smoke. (Isaiah 6:1–4)

The glory that was revealed to Isaiah puts everything else in the world to shame by comparison; the apostle John tells us in John 12 that it was Jesus who was sitting on that throne.

Until you are utterly convinced of God's infinite greatness, your trial, which is not even remotely comparable to his greatness, will seem bigger than he is. In order to suffer so as to profit most by God's grace in your sufferings, you need to read and pray and meditate until you are utterly convinced of God's infinite greatness.

4. Determine to remember the mystery of God's providence.

When we experience suffering, we always want to know why. We've seen that God knows we are prone to ask that question. That is why he lets that question be asked in the Bible, and that is why he gives us general answers. Yet there are always questions to which we cannot get as full an answer as we would like. In those instances it is vital for us to remember the mystery of

God's providence toward us. We do not always know what God is doing. So Paul exclaims in Romans 11:33–36:

> Oh, the depth of the riches and wisdom and knowledge of God! How unsearchable are his judgments and how inscrutable his ways!
>
> "For who has known the mind of the Lord,
>   or who has been his counselor?"
> "Or who has given a gift to him
>   that he might be repaid?"
>
> For from him and through him and to him are all things. To him be glory forever. Amen.

Paul is acknowledging that you can't always comprehend the judgments of God, and you can't always see the purposes of God. You don't always have the answers to all your questions *why?*

Job wasn't even given the answers that we read in the book of Job! It's important to remember that Job did not have the book of Job to read! He didn't have chapters 1 and 2, or chapter 42. He didn't know the background to his trial and testing. Nor could he have known the final conclusion of it. All he could do was trust God, who "moves in a mysterious way, his wonders to perform," who "plants his footsteps on the sea, and rides upon the storm."[1]

Remembering the mystery of God's providence redirects our attention from *why* to *God*. Though *we* seek comfort in answers to our question of *why* we suffer, *God* brings us comfort by answering the question of *who* is working mysteriously in our suffering.

It would be impossible for me to answer all of your questions about suffering, but I can tell you, beyond the shadow of a doubt, that you can find immovable and unshakable hope in the Lord Jesus Christ. When we turn our eyes from questions of *why* to worship, we are able to say, "You, O Lord, are what it's all about. I was made for you. Nothing can separate me from you in Christ Jesus. Neither tribulation, nor death, nor famine, nor nakedness, nor peril, nor sword, nor powers, nor principalities, nor height nor depth, nor any other created thing can separate me from *you*!"

5. Take account of your own sinfulness.

If you and I are going to profit most in our suffering by God's grace, we will need to take account of our own sinfulness. Isn't it interesting that Isaiah responds to the vision of the Lord by saying, "Woe is me! For I am lost; for I am a man of unclean lips, and I dwell in the midst of a people of unclean lips; for my eyes have seen the King, the LORD of hosts!" (Isaiah 6:5)? In light of the majesty of God, Isaiah becomes aware of his own sinfulness. Acknowledging our sin is vitally important so that Satan doesn't use it against us. We can realistically own the problems that we are causing ourselves. Sometimes we are the cause of our suffering. Sometimes we intensify our pain because of our sinful attitudes in response to suffering we haven't caused. Either way, our sin gets involved. It is important for us to recognize where our responsibility lies.

A few years ago, at a pastor's conference, two veteran ministers were asked, "How do you deal with criticism in your church?" The two veteran pastors exhorted the men just to soldier on without being discouraged and to trust in the Lord to vindicate them. A third pastor, however, when asked to comment, said, "Well, I think that one thing you might want to do if you are being criticized is consider that it might be right!" That is very wise advice.

Sometimes our personal sin brings about the suffering that we face. Other times, our sin exacerbates the suffering that began through no fault of our own. It is, therefore, good to consider our sinfulness in the midst of suffering.

6. Settle it in your heart that there is both a need and a purpose in your suffering.

The apostle Peter says,

In this you rejoice, though now for a little while, if necessary, you have been grieved by various trials, so that the tested genuineness of your faith—more precious than gold that perishes though it is tested by fire—may be found to result in praise and glory and honor at the revelation of Jesus Christ. (1 Peter 1:6–7)

Peter is saying that the testing that the believer experiences is going to be proven at the coming of Jesus Christ. Your suffering is going to produce in you, by God's grace and by God's Spirit, something that is worth far more than gold, something that lasts for all eternity. Settle it in your heart that there is both a need and a purpose for your suffering.

7. Believe in God's kind providence toward you.

In Revelation 3:19, God says, "Those whom I love, I reprove and discipline." That same truth is found in Hebrews:

And have you forgotten the exhortation that addresses you as sons?

"My son, do not regard lightly the discipline of
the Lord,
nor be weary when reproved by him.
For the Lord disciplines the one he loves,
and chastises every son whom he receives."

It is for discipline that you have to endure. God is treating you as sons. For what son is there whom his father does not discipline? If you are left without discipline, in which all have participated, then you are illegitimate children and not sons. Besides this, we have had earthly fathers who disciplined us and we respected them. Shall we not much more be subject to the Father of spirits and live? For they disciplined us for a short time as it seemed best to them, but he disciplines us for our good, that we may share his holiness. For the moment all discipline seems painful rather than pleasant, but later it yields the peaceful fruit of righteousness to those who have been trained by it. (Hebrews 12:5–11)

Believe in God's kind providence toward you in suffering. His purposes are for your good and demonstrate his love. In the midst of suffering, remember that God is calling you his son or daughter.

Study Questions

1. In one way or another, suffering is the result of living in a fallen world. What does Paul say in Galatians 5:17 and Romans 7:14–25 that may help us understand the cause of our suffering? How might our suffering prove beneficial in this connection?

2. God can use suffering in the life of believers for many spiritual benefits if we humble ourselves to learn and submit to his teaching. What does Scripture say about how God works in us through our suffering and pain (Philippians 3:10; Hebrews 12:5–6; 12:10–11)?

3. To humble ourselves and trust God in difficult circumstances, we must believe in and rely upon his power. The Bible gives many evidences of the power of God over the world, mankind, and the devil. What are some of those evidences?

    a. Romans 1:4; Ephesians 1:19–20
    b. Romans 8:11; Ephesians 2:5–6; Colossians 2:13
    c. 1 Corinthians 15:24–27
    d. 2 Peter 3:13; Revelation 21:5

4. God's power gives us freedom to face suffering by transforming us. What does that look like (Mark 10:42–45; John 10:17–18; 13:1; Philippians 2:5ff.)?

4

WHAT SHOULD WE THINK OF JESUS' SUFFERING?

DID JESUS have to suffer, too? Or better yet, did Jesus, the sinless Son of Man, have to experience human suffering far beyond the experience of any other? As difficult as this question is even to ask, it is something that Scripture testifies to from Genesis to Revelation.

Have you ever thought about that? God starts talking about Jesus' sufferings in the book of Genesis? Jesus' sufferings were recorded in Scripture fifteen hundred years before he was born. One of the most beautiful and elaborate and detailed and explicit descriptions of his life and the sufferings it entailed was written by the prophet Isaiah over six hundred years before Jesus was born. Likewise, the Gospels and the letters of the New Testament recount in detail the suffering of the Lord Jesus Christ and his response to it. As Christians, we are explicitly asked to look at Jesus' sufferings and learn about our own suffering, which is precisely what we are going to do.

THE BIBLE FROM THE BEGINNING SPEAKS OF JESUS' SUFFERING

The first explicit thing that the Bible tells us about Jesus is his victory over Satan. In Genesis 3:15, God is speaking to the devil about Jesus, and he says, "He shall bruise your head," indicating a fatal blow to Satan. The very first thing that God says about Jesus, the coming Messiah, is that he's going to win. Jesus is going to destroy Satan and all his works.

But do you know the second thing God says about Jesus? It is that he is going to suffer. Jesus will suffer at the hands of the very one that he is going to crush. Even as he will have victory over that Serpent, he is going to suffer by its fangs. The Serpent will bruise him in the heel—the point being that though Jesus will have ultimate victory, yet the Serpent is going to wound him. The first thing that is said about Jesus by God in the Bible is that he will win, but the second thing is that he will suffer.

WHY JESUS WAS CALLED "A MAN OF SORROWS, ACQUAINTED WITH GRIEF"

Isaiah 53 says:

Who has believed what he has heard from us?
> And to whom has the arm of the LORD been
>> revealed?
For he grew up before him like a young plant,
> and like a root out of dry ground;
he had no form or majesty that we should look at him,
> and no beauty that we should desire him.
He was despised and rejected by men;
> a man of sorrows, and acquainted with grief;
and as one from whom men hide their faces
> he was despised, and we esteemed him not.

Surely he has borne our griefs
> and carried our sorrows;
yet we esteemed him stricken,
> smitten by God, and afflicted.
But he was wounded for our transgressions;
> he was crushed for our iniquities;

upon him was the chastisement that brought us
    peace,
  and with his stripes we are healed.
All we like sheep have gone astray;
  we have turned—every one—to his own way;
and the LORD has laid on him
  the iniquity of us all.

He was oppressed, and he was afflicted,
  yet he opened not his mouth;
like a lamb that is led to the slaughter,
  and like a sheep that before its shearers is silent,
  so he opened not his mouth.
By oppression and judgment he was taken away;
  and as for his generation, who considered
that he was cut off out of the land of the living,
  stricken for the transgression of my people?
And they made his grave with the wicked
  and with a rich man in his death,
although he had done no violence,
  and there was no deceit in his mouth.

Yet it was the will of the LORD to crush him;
  he has put him to grief;
when his soul makes an offering for guilt,
  he shall see his offspring; he shall prolong his
    days;
the will of the LORD shall prosper in his hand.

Out of the anguish of his soul he shall see and be
    satisfied;
by his knowledge shall the righteous one, my
    servant,
    make many to be accounted righteous,
    and he shall bear their iniquities.
Therefore I will divide him a portion with the
    many,
    and he shall divide the spoil with the strong,
because he poured out his soul to death
    and was numbered with the transgressors;
yet he bore the sin of many,
    and makes intercession for the transgressors.

You may be tempted to respond, "How do you
know that this is about Jesus? His name isn't even
mentioned anywhere in this passage." Acts 8 offers a
reply. It tells of an Ethiopian royal official in his chariot
who was reading this passage when, providentially,
he happened upon Philip the evangelist. "And the
eunuch said to Philip, 'About whom, I ask you, does
the prophet say this, about himself or about someone
else?' Then Philip opened his mouth, and beginning
with this Scripture he told him the good news about
Jesus" (Acts 8:34–35). No wonder the Ethiopian official was confused by that passage. Even Christians are
blown away when they hear this description about the
Servant of the Lord. This is not what people were

expecting of God's own Son, the anointed one sent into the world for the salvation of sinners.

Recently I reread an article, "The Emotional Life of Our Lord," which I probably read for the first time twenty or twenty-five years ago. It was written by the brilliant scholar B. B. Warfield, who taught at Princeton Theological Seminary. He was a great defender of the inspiration, authority, and inerrancy of Scripture and a great advocate for the deity of Christ and other cardinal doctrines of Christianity. The article is about sixty pages of dense reflection on what the New Testament teaches us about the emotional state of our Lord Jesus Christ in his earthly walk. After surveying the evidence, Warfield says this:

> Of the lighter pleasurable emotions that flit across the mind in response to appropriate incitements arising occasionally in the course of social intercourse, we also hear little in the case of Jesus. It is not once recorded that he laughed; we do not ever hear even that he smiled; only once are we told that he was glad, and then it is rather sober gratification than exuberant delight which is spoken of in connection with him (Jno. xi. 15). But, then, we hear little also of his passing sorrows. The sight of Mary and her companions wailing at the tomb of Lazarus, agitated his soul and caused him tears (Jno. xi. 35) ; the stubborn unbelief of Jerusalem drew from him loud wailing (Lk. xix. 41). He sighed at

the sight of human suffering (Mk. vii. 34) and "sighed deeply" over men's hardened unbelief (viii. 12): man's inhumanity to man smote his heart with pain (iii. 5). But it is only with reference to his supreme sacrifice that his mental sufferings are emphasized.[1]

I share this with you not to paint a picture of a grim, morose, brooding Lord Jesus; after all, what does he say to his disciples just prior to his death? "These things I have spoken to you, that my joy may be in you, and that your joy may be full" (John 15:11). Nevertheless, Jesus was a man of sorrows and acquainted with grief.

As a Man of Sorrows, He Is Able to Sympathize

What do we make of the fact that he was a man of sorrows, acquainted with grief? Simply this, since Jesus was a man of sorrows and acquainted with grief, he is able to sympathize with us in all that we endure and experience in this fallen world. This is precisely what the Bible tells us.

Therefore he had to be made like his brothers in every respect, so that he might become a merciful and faithful high priest in the service of God, to make propitiation for the sins of the people. For because he himself has suffered when tempted, he is able to help those who are being tempted. (Hebrews 2:17–18)

Since then we have a great high priest who has passed through the heavens, Jesus, the Son of God, let us hold fast our confession. For we do not have a high priest who is unable to sympathize with our weaknesses, but one who in every respect has been tempted as we are, yet without sin. Let us then with confidence draw near to the throne of grace, that we may receive mercy and find grace to help in time of need. (Hebrews 4:14–16)

There are some people in this world who are so intimidated by the thought of approaching Jesus directly that they feel a need to go to someone else to do it on their behalf. After all, how could they ever approach the almighty, sinless, Son of God by themselves? But you need to understand something. The author of Hebrews says that Jesus is the best high priest who ever lived. Whereas the earthly high priest had to offer a sacrifice for his own sins, Jesus did not, because he was perfect.

JESUS SYMPATHIZES *BETTER* THAN A SINFUL, EARTHLY HIGH PRIEST

Jesus, who never sinned, is more able to sympathize with you in your trials, in your temptations, and in your sufferings, than a fellow sinner is. That is a shocking statement, isn't it?

Warfield's article, "The Emotional Life of Our Lord," says that the thing that the Gospels emphasize most about our Lord Jesus' emotional state is his compassion. Everywhere he turns, he is filled with compassion.

Isn't that exactly what we should expect in light of Hebrews 4:14–16? In fact, that is exactly what the Gospels reveal to us. Immediately after Jesus' cousin, John the Baptist, was beheaded at the behest of an immoral young woman and a lecherous old king, Jesus was ministering to a crowd that was hungry. These people were probably unaware of the things that were taking place in Jesus' life, yet he looked on them, "and he had compassion" (Mark 6:34). Sinners tend to be self-centered, but Jesus is free to be compassionate, because in him there is no vileness and no sin.

When Jesus was on a hillside looking down on Jerusalem, he said, "O Jerusalem, Jerusalem, the city that kills the prophets and stones those who are sent to it! How often would I have gathered your children together as a hen gathers her brood under her wings, and you would not!" (Luke 13:34). He had compassion on sinners!

In John 11, when Mary and Martha were weeping over Lazarus's death, Jesus wept in compassion (verse 35). Over and over the Gospels drive home his compassion. His suffering, dare we say, worked and

71

manifested a compassion in him the likes of which the world has never seen.

What Hebrews 4:14–16 tells us is extraordinary. The passage is emphasizing the greatness of Christ and, at the same time, his sympathy. The juxtaposition of the greatness of Christ and the sympathy of Christ is actually jarring.

The divine Son is sympathetic to us. Who better to sympathize with you in your sufferings than your mother or your father, or your husband or your wife, or your son or your daughter, or your dearest friend in life? Perhaps it is those friends who are going through the same thing as you who are particularly helpful. Who is it that turns out to be more sympathetic than all of them put together and rolled into one? The one who is the heir of all things! The one who made the world! The one who is the radiance of God's glory! The one who upholds all things by the word of his power. The one who is a high priest according to the order of Melchizedek, who has passed through the heavens. The one who lived in sinless perfection, perfection beyond the holy angels. The one who endured suffering although he was the very Son of God. Jesus Christ is the one who sympathizes with you more and better than anyone or everyone else in the world.

Perhaps that is why the author of Hebrews expresses Jesus' sympathy in the form of a denial. He does not simply say that he is able to sympathize with you; instead, he says he's "not unable" to sympathize with you. You might be tempted to think that he is not able to sympathize with you, and perhaps that is why he says it that way.

WE HAVE A MEDIATOR WHO UNDERSTANDS OUR PROBLEMS

The author of Hebrews argues that the range of our Savior's temptation and suffering is universal. We have "one who in every respect has been tempted as we are" (Hebrews 4:15).

This phrase answers many questions: How can Jesus sympathize with me? How could it be that one so holy, so perfect, could sympathize with a poor, wretched, inconsistent sinner like me? How can Christ, the glorious, obedient high priest, sympathize with your weaknesses and mine? How can he possibly know my struggles with sin? How can he possibly know how I feel in my temptation and trial and suffering? How can he possibly know these things? *He was tempted in all things as we are.*

By the way, that does not mean that Christ has experienced every specific temptation that every specific believer faces. Christ, for instance, never gave birth to

73

a child, and I am told that there are some discomforts associated with that particular activity! Nevertheless, his experience of trial, testing, temptation, and suffering is actually broader than yours. Even if he has not been tested identically in every situation that you have experienced, his experience of suffering is actually broader than yours.

Although we could enumerate many parallels between his experience and ours, the emphasis of Hebrews is on the temptation, which he endured in his suffering. "For because he himself has suffered when tempted, he is able to help those who are being tempted" (Hebrews 2:18). Hebrews 5:8 says, "Although he was a son, he learned obedience through what he suffered." That is, his obedience was not an easy obedience. His obedience and temptation cost him dearly.

Briefly, we need to consider three aspects of his suffering: he suffered with us; he suffered without us; he suffered for us.

He Suffered with Us

First, Jesus suffers with you and me. Whatever you are suffering right now, Jesus has been there. We could think of the likeness of his temptation and ours, but there are so many other points of contact. For instance, are you getting to that age where your feet are never warm? He knew what it meant to be cold. Have you ever been hungry, really hungry? I'm not sure I have. He, however, knew both hunger and thirst. Have you ever had your house taken away from you in embarrassing and humiliating and depressing circumstances? He never owned a home. In fact, Jesus told his disciples that he did not even have a place of his own to lay his head. Have you ever been anguished deep in your soul, beside yourself, not having the slightest idea where to turn? John tells us that on the eve of his crucifixion his soul was "deeply troubled"—his grief was even to the point of death.

Have you ever been afraid? Or so sad that you thought you would never smile again? He knew fear and sorrow. Have you ever been afraid of death? He dreaded the cup of God's wrath that he had agreed to drink from the foundation of the world. You can see the escalating extremity of his temptation. He began his career of suffering for us in the manger, and it continued in his ministry through Gethsemane and Golgotha.

In all these ways, his suffering has so many points of contact with your sufferings that you can say, "The Bible shows that Jesus suffered like this too. He literally understands what I am going through here in this place. He has felt the same emotion that I am feeling right now. My Savior, my God, knows what it is like to be inside my skin, inside my head, inside my heart, and to feel the way that I am feeling right now." Jesus has suffered with you.

He Suffered without Us

Second, Jesus suffered without us. We may be tempted to think that Christ cannot understand our particular situation. We may assume that there is some point of discontinuity between our experience and his that makes it impossible for him to really sympathize with us. But here is the glorious news. It is precisely because there is a discontinuity between your experience and Jesus' experience that he is able to sympathize with you in all things. In fact, Jesus has experienced something that, by God's grace, the Christian will never have to experience.

You could spend an eternity in heaven and never meet a person who experienced being utterly forsaken by God—except Jesus Christ. He's the only person in heaven who knows what it is to have the Father turn his back on him, leaving him all alone. He is the only person in heaven who knows what it is to look down into the white-hot volcano of the wrath of God and survive. If you are a Christian, you will never know what that is like. Since he experienced something that you will, by God's grace, never experience, he is able to sympathize with you in everything.

In fact, the question is not whether he can sympathize with you in everything. The question is, can you sympathize with him in everything? No, you can't. You'll spend eternity in heaven, and you will never know what it was like for your Savior to do what he did for you. The cross will just get bigger and bigger and bigger and bigger, all eternity long. You'll love him more and more and more, because you'll go deeper and deeper and deeper into what he has done for you, and you'll never get to the bottom, because you can't enter into his experience. Although he suffered with you, he also suffered without you. You weren't there. The answer to the question that the old spiritual asks, "Were you there when they crucified my Lord?" is, "No! I was not. He was absolutely alone. Everyone left him. They all abandoned him. He was alone. No! I wasn't there when they crucified my Lord. He did that without me."

He Suffered for Us

Third, Jesus suffered for us. Understand that Jesus didn't come into this world, so that he could empathize with you. When your car is broken down, and you've got the hood up with your hands covered in oil, Jesus is not like the person who comes along and says, "Hmm? Problem with your car? Oh, so sorry about that. That must be really frustrating to have a problem with your car. And it's raining, to boot! I'll bet you're soaking wet, aren't you?" All the while, they're standing under an umbrella talking to you! "Bet you're cold. Hmm. I feel your pain, you know? Really do. Look, I'm late for an appointment—gotta go."

Jesus did not come to empathize with you in your suffering. Jesus came to bear your suffering. Get this if you don't get anything else. Jesus came to bear a punishment that would have destroyed you.

Jesus did not do it by coming alongside you and experiencing the wrath of God with you. He came, pushed you behind his back, and said, "Father, I'll take this for them." You don't know what Christ endured for you, because he bore the wrath of God so that you might not have to.

I love the way one Christian puts this: "In Jesus' suffering for you, your debt was not cancelled. It was liquidated." The heavenly Father did not look down on what Jesus was doing on the cross and say, "Okay, okay. I'm just going to forget that they owed me. We are just going to call that off. No more debt owed. I am just going to pretend like they never incurred that debt. Just forgive it." Jesus, rather, paid your debt to the last drop, and then said, in effect, "Father, I have bought them with my blood. Now they belong to me, and no one in the world can take them from my pierced hands."

Do you see why Christians cannot conceive of standing before God at the end of time, and saying, "Look, Jesus is just fine. Love him. Great teaching. Sweet, dear man. He really loved people. But, look, I have tried to live a good life, and I would like to go to heaven now. I don't need Jesus. He's nice. Learned a lot from him, but I've tried to live a good life. I can come in here on my own"?

Christians can't do that, because they know that Jesus paid for their sin to the last drop with his own blood. All that he suffered, he suffered in their place. The Christian's suffering in this life, then, is nothing compared to what it would have been were it not for the Lord Jesus Christ. When it is as bad as it can possibly be, it is never as bad as it ought to be, because he has suffered for us. In the hardest places of our lives, in the deepest suffering and the darkest hours and the blackest nights, in times when sorrow and tribulation overwhelm your very souls, and you feel as if the Lord cannot hear your cry, you are never standing where Jesus stood.

He stood there, not with you, but for you, in your stead. You can never stand where he stood, and you can never understand what he bore—never—because he

79

not only shared with you in suffering; he has endured suffering and tribulation in your place. That is why the author of Hebrews can say that he is a great high priest who is able to sympathize with us and have compassion on us.

What Should We Learn from This?

We are supposed to look at Jesus' sufferings and learn something. "For to this you have been called, because Christ also suffered for you, leaving you an example, so that you might follow in his steps" (1 Peter 2:21). We are supposed to learn something about our suffering.

> Since therefore Christ suffered in the flesh, arm yourselves with the same way of thinking, for whoever has suffered in the flesh has ceased from sin, so as to live for the rest of the time in the flesh no longer for human passions but for the will of God. For the time that is past suffices for doing what the Gentiles want to do, living in sensuality, passions, drunkenness, orgies, drinking parties, and lawless idolatry. (1 Peter 4:1–3)

Later Peter says, "After you have suffered a little while, the God of all grace, who has called you to his eternal glory in Christ, will himself restore, confirm, strengthen, and establish you" (1 Peter 5:10–11). Although there are a lot of things that we are to learn from the sufferings of Christ, we will only focus on four.

Draw a Line from Our Suffering Back to Sin

As we saw above, we must learn to draw a line from our suffering back to sin, because one of God's purposes in suffering, as we look at the death of Christ, is to cause us to learn to hate sin like we hate suffering.

Recently, I was talking with a woman who remembers the first time she saw a family with their Down syndrome child. When she saw the child fall on the sidewalk, she remembers thinking that they were facing a life of caring for a sweet child who would never be able to reach her human potential and care for herself in the way that other adults do. Her heart was overwhelmed with sorrow at the thought of what that little child would endure, a child who could have been any number of amazing things. The parents were forced to live every day wondering, "What's going to happen to my child after I'm gone?"

Although this family's trial was probably unrelated to their sin, their struggle reflects the fact that sin has entered this world. God wants us to look at suffering in this world, draw a line back to sin, and learn to hate the sin like we hate the suffering. As you look at something that causes you to hate suffering, do you hate sin like you hate that suffering? If you are anything like me, you do not. I hate suffering far more than I hate sin. But I want to learn to hate sin like God hates sin. If we will draw a line from suffering and misery back to sin, we will grow in learning how to hate sin.

Draw a Line from Our Suffering Back to Jesus

We need to draw a line from our suffering back to Jesus so that we say, "Lord, this suffering is beyond anything that I've ever endured, but Jesus' suffering was far worse than this." Turning our thoughts from our suffering to Christ's will cause us to treasure his suffering all the more. This puts our suffering in perspective, as we say, in effect, "Father, if I struggle to put one foot in front of another in this situation, how must my Lord Jesus have felt, living his life with the conscious knowledge that he was headed for the cross! He did it willingly for me. This moment is hard enough for me, and I didn't have to think about it till now." Our suffering enables us to treasure Jesus' sufferings more and puts our suffering in perspective.

I do not want to belittle our suffering! The way we cope with our suffering is not so much by saying, "Oh, it's not so bad," because sometimes it is absolutely terrible. The way to cope with our suffering is not to minimize it, but to realize the depth of Jesus' sufferings. We can look honestly in the mirror and say, "Yes, it is terrible, but Jesus' sufferings were greater." Such a transforming attitude will inevitably lead to worship.

Draw a Line from Our Suffering to the Body of Jesus

The apostle Paul tells us that his suffering was for building up the body of Christ, that is, the church, his household, his family, his people. If we are believers in the Lord Jesus Christ, our suffering is meant to be edifying for our family, with whom we will share blissful eternity, those with whom we now walk through a fallen world filled with deep pain and great distress and suffering. Our suffering is, at least in part, for the welfare and good and edification of our brothers and sisters in Christ. God does not plan to waste your suffering (that is, he plans for you to grow through your suffering), and neither does he intend to waste your suffering on his other children either. He intends for the church to be edified corporately by the suffering of its members.

When you read a missionary biography, pausing to think of the sacrifice of another believer for the sake of the gospel, you are edified by that example. It may even be that you were brought to Christ through the sacrifice and loss of others. The Lord often sends his people out to die, metaphorically, if not literally, but through the ashes of their loss he brings life. God manifests, to us and to the whole body, his power in our weakness.

Draw a Line from Our Suffering to Its Purposes

Finally, we need to draw a line from our suffering to its goals and purposes. Everything we have talked about pertains to this, but I especially want to come back to what B. B. Warfield said about Jesus. What is the emotion ascribed to Jesus more than any other in the Gospels? *Compassion.*

If Jesus—a man of sorrows, who was acquainted with grief—was a man of compassion, what should our suffering create in us? Compassion! If Jesus in his suffering displayed compassion, should not our suffering achieve its goal of making us not only God-loving, Christ-treasuring, gospel-believing, godliness-pursuing Christians, but also compassionate Christians? Since we have gone through the valley of suffering, shouldn't we be tender and forgiving and caring, longing to live as Christ lived, forgiving as Christ forgave, and caring as Christ cared?

One of the chief goals of our suffering is to make us more compassionate. The ultimate goal of all our lives, whether in times of pleasure or of pain, is to glorify God. We do that as we are drawn closer to him in the midst of our suffering. His compassion becomes ours. We too are able to sympathize with others in their weakness. And others will see in us the glory of Christ, in and through our suffering.

Grace does grow best in winter.

STUDY QUESTIONS

1. In a day when people are drawn to a religion that promotes happiness and self-actualization, note how the apostles focused on Christ and his suffering as the key to evangelism (Acts 2:23; 3:18; 17:3; 26:22–23). Why was it necessary to explain Christ's suffering, and how can we learn from their example?

2. Why was it necessary for Christ to suffer?

3. What are some ways Christ suffered that are similar to the ways you suffer?

4. What are some ways Christ suffered that you never will? How does that affect your current suffering?

5. How do you respond to suffering that is the result of your own sin?

6. How do you respond to the suffering that is the result of someone else's sin?

7. What have you learned about Jesus' suffering that can help you in the two previous questions?

NOTES

Chapter 1: Why Me?

1. Much of this chapter is influenced by the writings of John Piper, including his April 30, 2003, article "Suffering, Mercy, and Heavenly Regret," http://www.desiringgod.org/ResourceLibrary/TasteAndSee/ByDate/2003/1234_Suffering_Mercy_and_Heavenly_Regret.

Chapter 3: How Can We Profit from Suffering?

1. From the hymn, "God Moves in a Mysterious Way" by William Cowper.

Chapter 4: What Should We Think of Jesus' Suffering?

1. Benjamin B. Warfield, "The Emotional Life of Our Lord," *The Person and Work of Christ* (Philadelphia: Presbyterian and Reformed, 1968), 126–27.

Ligon Duncan (MDiv, MA, Covenant Theological Seminary; PhD, University of Edinburgh) is senior minister of the historic First Presbyterian Church of Jackson, Mississippi. He formerly was the John R. Richardson professor of systematic theology at Reformed Theological Seminary. He is the president and chairman of the council of the Alliance of Confessing Evangelicals, as well as the Chairman of the Council on Biblical Manhood and Womanhood.

Pastor Duncan is the author or coauthor of several books, among them *Fear Not*, *The Genesis Debate*, and *Women's Ministry in the Local Church*.

J. Nicholas Reid (MDiv, Reformed Theological Seminary, Jackson) is the senior minister's assistant at First Presbyterian Church, Jackson, Mississippi. He is a coauthor of *Fear Not*, associate editor of *The Westminster Confession into the 21st Century*, volume 3, and associate editor of Reformed Academic Press.

Where Is God in All of This?
Finding God's Purpose in Our Suffering
Deborah Howard

$9.99, paper, 160 pages
ISBN: 978-1-59638-124-7

Deborah Howard, an experienced hospice nurse and counselor, draws from her experiences with the doubts of suffering, anguished, and questioning people and reminds us that all things happen for good, God-glorifying purposes.

"Just what suffering people need: thirteen simple yet profound biblical reasons why God brings suffering our way.... Deborah Howard lifts us above our self-centered murmuring to focus on God and our real spiritual profit. Read this remarkable book yourself... before suffering crosses your path, and give a copy to every suffering person you know." —JOEL BEEKE

"Warm, wise, kind, honest, and full of the Word, helpfully applied! Thanks to Deborah for writing it." —BOB LEPINE

Treasures in Darkness
A Grieving Mother Shares Her Heart
Sharon W. Betters

$13.99, paper, 277 pages
ISBN: 978-0-87552-798-7

"In twenty years of women's ministry, I have never read such a compelling, painfully real, transparent perspective on grief. Sharon Betters brings hope to a broken heart in the midst of profound loss." —**Tammy Maltby**

"Betters's world turned upside down when her son died in an automobile accident. She tells her story with candor, honesty, and hope." —**Rose Marie Miller**

"No hope is real if it fails to recognize the reality of the pain and the necessity of pressing through darkness with nothing but faith to find our way. Sharon squarely faces personal pain and tenderly offers the realities of faith to provide a journey to hope even through our darkest nights." —**Bryan Chapell**

Why Does It Have to Hurt?
The Meaning of Christian Suffering
DAN G. MCCARTNEY

$9.99, paper, 144 pages
ISBN: 978-0-87552-386-6

If God is all-powerful and all-good, why do Christians suffer?

"Dan McCartney's splendid book . . . has all the qualities necessary to help us deal with such a sensitive, personal, and often difficult question. It is thoroughly honest and realistic; its approach is marked by Christian wisdom; and above all, it is biblical—and set out in his clear, readable, and easily followed style." —SINCLAIR B. FERGUSON

"I grow tired of books on suffering which either ignore the real problem or offer clichés as answers to the problem of suffering. Dan McCartney has done neither. He looks the 'monster' in the eye and, with Bible in hand, gives honest answers to honest questions about suffering. This is a refreshing book." —STEVE BROWN

Living in the Hope of Glory
ADOLPHE MONOD

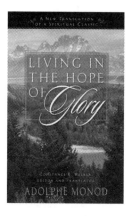

$12.99, paper, 179 pages
ISBN: 978-0-87552-568-6

"Adolphe Monod was one of the greatest French preachers of the 19th century. Struck with terminal cancer, he presented from his bed a meditation on the last twenty-five Sundays of his life. This has been a French devotional classic since 1856. By virtue of Constance Walker's translation, 'though dead, yet he speaks.'" —ROGER NICOLE

"It is astonishing that Monod's *Les Adieux* are not better known to the wider world. This courageous French Reformed pastor was both passionate in his care for people and singular in his devotion to God." —WILLIAM EDGAR

"Instructing, enriching, and inspiring. Here, the suffering Christian will find an uplifting companion." —RICHARD D. PHILLIPS

Suffering
Eternity Makes a Difference
PAUL DAVID TRIPP

$2.99, paper, 40 pages
ISBN: 978-0-87552-684-3

How hard it is to see God's goodness in the face of tragedy and suffering! Feeling abandoned, we cry out to him, question him, turn away from him, perhaps even curse him. It may seem like he's cheated us—we've done our part following him, but he's let us down.

Paul David Tripp helps hurting people see their circumstances from an eternal perspective. Gently uncovering the wrong motives, faulty reasoning, and misguided conclusions that can blind us to the truth of God's love and goodness, Tripp focuses us on the grand picture of eternity. His compassionate approach and scriptural advice will help bring strength and hope to grieving souls.

Give Praise to God
A Vision for Reforming Worship
EDITED BY PHILIP GRAHAM RYKEN, DEREK W. H. THOMAS, AND J. LIGON DUNCAN III

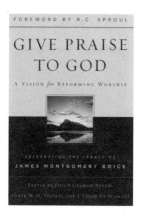

$29.99, cloth, 536 pages
ISBN: 978-87552-553-2

These essays by some of the leading advocates of Reformed worship examine the biblical foundations for worship, the warranted elements of corporate worship, worship in the home and in all of life, and worship throughout the ages.

"Sanctified scholarship, solid biblical content, and warm pastoral application. . . . I found my mind being stretched and my heart stirred." —ALISTAIR BEGG

"A worthy tribute of love and honor to the memory of James Montgomery Boice. In it a galaxy of his colleagues and friends address the theme that was the heartbeat of his life and ministry. The contributors offer important instruction, insight, and challenge on the grand theme of worship." —SINCLAIR B. FERGUSON

Should We Leave Our Churches?
A Biblical Response to Harold Camping
J. LIGON DUNCAN AND MARK R. TALBOT

$5.99, paper, 48 pages
ISBN: 978-0-87552-788-8

Harold Camping, president of the Family Radio Network, has announced that the church age has come to an end. He claims that God is no longer blessing local churches and that all Christians should leave their congregations.

How should Christians respond? Ligon Duncan and Mark Talbot clearly set forth what the Bible says about the church.

"Camping's teaching on the end of the church age is a poisonous heresy. This book is the perfect antidote. It will help people who have encountered Camping to understand why his teaching is false. More positively, it explains the true nature of the church and the way God uses it for our spiritual good. An ideal book to read and to share with others." —PHILIP GRAHAM RYKEN